Who am I?

Alan Rommelfanger

WHO AM I?

Spiritual Reflections on Life

CKBooks Publishing

No part of this book may be reproduced, scanned, or distributed in any print or electronic form without permission.
Contact: alanr380@outlook.com

ISBN : 978-0-9892152-7-5 (paperback)

Copyright © 2024 Alan Rommelfanger
All rights reserved.

All images are by Teresa DuChateau except on page 43 – by Alan Rommelfanger and page 55 – by ESA/Hubble & NASA
Vine image by Ganna Galata

Published by CKBooks Publishing
PO Box 214
New Glarus, WI, 53574
ckbookpublishing.com

For the grandchildren and
great-grandchildren

Contents

Introduction 1
The Quest 4
Companions 8
Ancestors 10
Relax 12
I Think 14
Go with the Flow 16
Two Images 20
Follow Your Path 22
Jonah 24
Mother Goddess 26
Finding the Way 28
Mother 32
Thy Kin-dom Come 34
The Dimension of Wholeness 36
Multiple Points of View 38
How do I See 40
My Mom 44
Religion 46
Centered Prayer 48

Evolution	50
The Past is Enfolded	52
All is One	56
Let Go	58
To Live is to Change	60
Who am I?	62
Sparks	64
Passive vs Active Belief	68
The Incarnation	70
The Kin-dom	72
Time	74
Trees	76
The Messiness of Change	80
Peace in Chaos	82
Doubt	84
Spiritual Experience and Religion	86
Prayer	88
Autumn	90
A version of the Lord's Prayer	94
There is More	96

Guns and Bullets	98
Do Trees Have Souls?	100
Wonder	102
Breath	106
Layers of Life	108
Nobody	110
Love	112
Parable of the Workers	114
Church	116
Prayers Change	118
The Cloud's Prayer	120
Acknowledgments	122
About the Author	123

Introduction

> *I was neither a prophet nor the son of a prophet, but I was a shepherd, and I also took care of sycamore-fig trees. But the LORD took me from tending the flock and said to me, 'Go, prophesy to my people Israel.*
>
> Amos 7:14-15 (NIV)

Like Amos, I am not a professional theologian or a trained pastor. I am trained as an engineer and my professional life was spent applying computers to business systems. I am a husband to my wife of fifty-six years and the father of six grown children.

Like Amos in his time, I feel that our time calls for prophets. We are all called to share our gifts and insights to help our planet and life upon it through the crisis that looms before us. Some have been called to awaken us to the crisis. However, my call is to share these reflections in the hope that they will remind us of who we are, not with answers but with questions.

If we have faith and are willing to tell ourselves new stories, a crisis can be an opportunity for growth and transformation. Growth and transformation of each of us as individuals and for the community of life on this planet Earth.

Alan Rommelfanger

*I am the vine; you are the branches.
If you remain in me and I in you,
you will bear much fruit.*

John 15:5

The Quest

I am on a journey
of self-discovery
and an exploration
of Reality.

It began
when Reality
brought me into being.

In each moment
it is sustained,
not by my efforts.
Although,
I can and must
make an effort.

It is sustained,
by the Creator
that holds all in existence.

Prayer:

Spirit of Life,
Live in me and through me
every moment of today.

Thank you for the gift of life.

I am on a journey
of self-discovery
and an exploration
of Reality.

Companions

We walk with people
for a portion of our journey.
The companions we have
are God's way of walking with us.
Our sharing with them
helps all of us to grow.

As I look back
all the way
to childhood,
there have been many,
who knowingly
and unknowingly,
have been God-companions
on my journey.

Prayer:

In each day
and every age
you are there,
sharing the journey into the future,
guiding my growth
and understanding
of you
and the journey.

Continue to walk with me,
Spirit of Companionship and Wisdom,
Help me to be a faithful companion,
to those who accompany me.

Ancestors

I need to honor,
and respect
my ancestors.

They have given me my flesh,
they have planted in me
the sacred stories
that are the basis of my personal story
and the roots of my values.

Yes, I have critiqued
and deepened my understanding of those stories.
I have expanded,
through education
and life experiences,
their meaning.

Prayer:

Thank you,
all who have gone before me,
parents, grandparents, great grandparents….
But also
the whole human family
and the larger family
of life on the Earth.

Please help me to make my contribution
to the work of creation.

Relax

To relax
is an act
of faith.

It takes trust
to truly relax.
Drop your guard.
Be at peace.
Let go of tension.
Allow yourself to be held
by Reality.

What is,
IS.
There is no need to change it.

Prayer:

Breathe in Love,
Breathe out all tension and anxiety.

Imagine yourself as an infant,
sitting in Mother's embrace.

I Think

John Descartes said,
"I think therefore I am."

But I was,
long before
I thought.

I "think"
my thoughts
stand in the way,
of being in touch
— face to face —
with my truest self.

I don't see a way
to think myself
out of this dilemma.

But I don't have to.

Relax and trust
the love
that brought me into being
and sustains me breath by breath.

Prayer:

Spirit of Life,
Help me to let go of my thoughts
and trust
Divine Love.

Go with the Flow

Life is not static,
it is a continuous process
of growth and transformation.

The egg,
with its well-shaped shell,
must crack and fall apart,
for the duckling to emerge.

A woman
must endure labor pains,
for a child to be born.

A seed
must soften and sprout,
for the plant to emerge and grow.

Don't abandon
the path that you're on.

Let it lead you
to the point of change.

It may be
death and rebirth.

It may be
a fork in the road
where you are free
to choose,

but until you arrive there,
walk forward
one day at a time,
one step after the other.

Remember,
you are never alone.
All of Creation is with you.

Prayer:

Breathe in, Breathe out.

The egg,
with its well-shaped
shell,
must crack and fall
apart,
for the new life to
emerge.

Two Images

*Come to me, all you who are weary and
burdened, and I will give you rest.*
Matthew 11:28

Come to me and I will give you rest.
Welcoming arms reach out
to embrace and hold close.
You are enfolded
and protected in a warm,
cozy place.

*And whoever does not carry their cross and
follow me cannot be my disciple.*
Luke 14:27

Follow me.
There is a separation.
The leader goes before,
and you must pick yourself up
and follow.

The way is safe.
The leader precedes you.
But,
it is not the same warm resting place.

Prayer:

Spirit of Life,
I thank you,
for times of rest and comfort.
Give me strength and assurance,
as I daily walk,
following the leader
sent to guide me.

Follow Your Path

Why did Jesus die?

Many
have attempted to answer this question,
and many more will add their thoughts in
the future.

As I reflect on Jesus,
his life and words,

I think
it was to be true
to his path.

The Path of Life,
on which he found himself.
As he says in his prayer
and again in the prayer
in the garden,
"Thy will be done."

As I look at my life,
my Path of Life
began long before I was born.

It is my job,
now that I am consciously aware and awake,
to attempt
to follow that path to
and through death.

To stay open to the Divine will,
regardless of where it leads me,
regardless of the
circumstances and experiences
I find myself facing.

As Jesus invited — Follow Me.

Jonah

I've been reflecting on the prophet Jonah.
A symbol for all prophets.
He was called by God
and sent to the people of Nineveh.
But he didn't want to go.

There have been times
I was called and said yes.
But have there also been times
when I, like Jonah, ran away from my call?

However,
as the story unfolds,
that didn't affect God's plan or God's call.

Eventually, he found himself in Nineveh.
And not only was he there,
but the people believed him and repented.
Not what he had anticipated.
The wrath of God
did not descend upon the city.

And then,
just to make the point,
the broom tree
where he rested and found shade,
was killed by a worm,
and he found himself sitting
in the sun and the heat.

Prayer:

Lord God, I don't have to fix the world;
I only need to allow you to fix me.
Help me to be attentive to your call
and to go where you send me,
leaving the results
to the work of your spirit.

Mother Goddess

Last night on the news, they shared the results of a study in which ninety-seven percent of the women indicated that they had experienced inappropriate sexual harassment. Last week, eight women were killed in Atlanta. This morning there was a story about a woman in London who was attacked and killed by a police officer while walking home at night. Her death has triggered a global demonstration.

As I reflect
on these events,
I see patriarchy,
and your suppression,
Goddess Mother,
as a root cause.

If we,
Western Society,
recognized You
as coequal
with the Father,
it would have
a significant effect upon us men.

Help us to see
our sisters
as the daughters of God
that they are.

Manifestations of the Divine
with all your feminine characteristics.

Help us to see
that sexual attraction
is a manifestation
of Divine love
and is to be honored.
It is not a doorway to violence.

Heal all of us!

Finding the Way

How do I know?
How do you know?

Abraham left his religion and culture
to follow his spiritual experience.
Jesus was one of many spiritual leaders in his time.
We remember him.
But were the others not sincere?
Were they not true to their path?

Saint Francis went against his father's
guidance and will.
He lived on the edge of society.
Today we recognize Francis and Claire
as Saints.

Scripture, our accepted Christian story,
says that God has written his law upon our hearts.
In Francis' time, were his parents and their
community authorities wrong?

There is a path for me,
using the tools of discernment
and the gifts that I have been given.
I can choose to try to follow it,

trusting that the guidance
and help I need
will be there,
even in the darkest of times.

It is my path.
You should follow your path.
And if we have the opportunity
to walk together for a part of the journey,
it is but another grace that we have been
given.

Prayer:

Spirit of the Life Journey,
Thank you
for all my companions.
Help all of creation
to walk in harmony
with the Creator's plan.

There are no villains,
simply different paths.

Don't abandon
the path that you're on.

Let it lead you
to the point of change.

Mother

There has been a separation, a wall, if you will, between me and my mother. That is not to say that we never connected. No, the wall came from others, the Catholic Church and probably also the Dutch Reformed Church. It also came from Mom's disability, her hearing loss.

But the separation from my physical mom is the physical reflection of the separation that exists between our culture and a feminine image of the Divine. Again, it's there, but not fully. We Catholics pray to Mary. But she's not divine, our male priests say. All Christians honor her to some extent as the "Mother of God." That is an interesting title. How can God's mother be human only and yet God is Divine?

I think that The Big Bang was the Divine orgasm that poured out love in all its forms. The created universe is the result of this act of Divine love. The Trinity, the God in relationship is Mother, Father, and all of creation.

Prayer:

Spirit of Love,
Help all of us
to repair and heal
our relationships.

Let love flow freely
through us in all its forms.

Thy Kin-dom Come

The Kin-dom is here.

Visible and present
throughout the universe.

It is only missing
in the consciousness
of the human family.

Maybe it takes an experience
like global warming
for us to pay attention
and recognize
how interconnected
all life and existence are
on this planet.

Maybe that awareness
will only come through
the great suffering
that is about to enfold the planet.

And then we will cry out.
"Where are you, O God?"

Yet when you send prophets,
and signs,
we are so much into our own ways
that we do not pay attention.

Prayer:

Spirit of the Earth,
Awaken all of us fully.
Give us the help we need
to avoid the worst of this tragedy.

Show each of us,
myself included,
the actions that we should take.

The Dimension of Wholeness

Like Russian dolls, there's a succession of holons within me. It occurred to me that when I sit for centered prayer and form an intention, it is at the level of my consciousness that the intention is formed. But the holons that constitute me also participate in that sit. I am unable to access their consciousness — but they are conscious — each from the organ through the cell, molecule, and atom — have a form of consciousness and awareness. How can they contribute to my life if they can't sense in some way what they need to do? How does an immune system ward off COVID if it's not awake and aware?

And yet they all participate with me when I sit in prayer. And if I sit in prayer, doesn't that also affect the larger holon I am a part of? For I too, am but one holon in the community of the human family.

We watched a movie on the Hubble telescope last week. During a quiet period, the astronomers aimed it for nine days at a dark region of the sky where there were no stars. When they processed the image, they were amazed to see thousands of points of light, each a galaxy of billions of stars. They were so far away that they could only be seen when the light was gathered for an extended period. And now I too am aware of these far-off galaxies that have been sending their light since the dawn of creation.

So, what effect does my sit have upon the family of mankind or the community of life here on planet Earth?

Prayer:

Thank you,
for opening my eyes
a bit more to the oneness
that you are.

Human, Star, Squirrel, Robin, Cloud,
we are all
contained within you,
and we all affect the whole.

Multiple Points of View

What was Jesus' purpose
in telling the parable
of the laborers in the vineyard?

Maybe he wanted to give us
another point of view,
another way to look at life
and the world in which we live,
to open our eyes
to God's way of looking at us.

Do I insist that
my narrow view
is the way to see the world?
OR
Do I try to also see it
from someone else's
point of view?

Prayer:

Spirit of Light,
Continue to help me
open my eyes.

Help me to learn
to see the world
through the eyes of others.

If I see them,
their eyes are
in my eyes.

All is inter-existent.

How do I See

I'm working on a cross-stitch. As I looked at it the other day, it struck me. It's just colored thread. Yet, I can watch as a picture of buildings, flowers, water, sky, and several boats emerge. Is the image on the canvas — or is it in my eye — my inner eye? I have read that indigenous people who have not been exposed to pictures cannot see the image in a photograph. We have learned to see pictures.

If I had the eye of an atom, what would I see? I live in a sea of atoms of all sizes, but I don't see them. I see the boundaries that I interact with. The walls, the trees, the chair, the birds, other people. But are they separate? Or is it my learned experience that separates them?

I breathe in the molecules of the air that surround me. I eat and digest food and drink water. How is it that my body knows how to extract the nutrients it needs from the food?

Prayer:

Spirit of Life,
Continue to open my eyes,
the inner eye
to the wonder of life and creation.

Help me to see
in ever more complete ways
the Oneness of All.

It's just colored thread.

Is the image on the
canvas
or is it in my eye?

My Mom

I was raised in what the Catholic Church at the time called a "mixed marriage." My Mom — in order to marry the man she had come to love — had to sign an agreement with the Catholic Church that her children would be raised Catholic. But my Mom could be stubborn, too. She signed the agreement and left the religious upbringing of her boys to my Dad. She refused to bridge this religious gap and continued to go with her family to the Dutch Reformed Church. Her father was a Deacon in that church, and she thought it would be a betrayal to her family and to the religion in which they raised her to make a change. At the time, both churches considered themselves "better," truer to Christianity, and even more acceptable to God. I remember the Catholic nuns telling me to pray for our mother's conversion so she could be in heaven with us. Such was the thinking of the day.

Thank you, God, for inspiring Pope John to call for the Vatican Council and its teachings. which provided a fuller recognition of the other Christian Churches. We still have much further to go, but slowly we are making progress and letting go of our institutional pride. Christianity is not belonging to an institution. It is hearing the call of Jesus and following the path of that call. This does not require any institution. Albeit the framework — teachings, and fellowship — of an institution can be helpful.

Prayer:

Spirit of Life,
Thanks for the lessons
Mom and Dad taught us.

Also, thanks
for the progress toward unity
that Christian churches have made.

Help all of us to open ourselves
to new possibilities
of healing and fuller unity.

Religion

Religion is a part of my core identity.
But what is religion?
At one time it was my tribe and its understanding of the Life Mystery:
stories, rituals, and moral-codes
shared in a community.

But what is religion today?
Today we decide which church or
community we will join,
even within the framework of a larger
religious institution.
Frequently, individuals choose the religion
that they will participate in
and how committed they will be
to that participation.

All of us, because of the plurality in society,
are exposed to many
of the traditional religions,
their teachings, rituals, and sacred stories.

The main characters
in many of our sacred stories
did not see religion as central to their lives.

They encountered the Divine,
and lived in that relationship.

Does religion connect me to the Divine?

I think religion can be a good starting point.
But I need to find my relationship,
my path, and follow it.
Maybe it's good that religion is losing its grip
on people.

Prayer:

Spirit of Life, Guide all of us on the path
that leads deeper into the Mystery.

Centered Prayer

Daily I practice.
Practice being the operative word.

Most days I sink into a quiet place,
from which I emerge
just before the timer goes off.

Who?
What is keeping track of the time?

Some days there's a "dream" in the quiet.
Some days it feels like I've fallen asleep.

And then
there are those days
when I never do succeed
in quieting
and letting go
of the flow of thoughts.

Prayer:

Spirit of Quiet Presence,
you are in me always.

There, with each breath
and every beat of my heart.

The Silent Presence of Creation
that underlies all that is.
Thank you!

Evolution

Are we more evolved
than our grandparents?
More, better, higher, terms that imply a value
judgment.

Evolution is not about
becoming more or better.
It is about adapting to a continuously
changing environment,
an environment that is
continually being created.

We are better adapted
to twenty-first-century life
than our grandparents would be;
however,
place us in their environment,
a hundred years ago,
and we would not do so well.

Judge not, lest you be judged.

We each walk our own path.
We all have our own wounds
that need to heal,
and our own gifts
that we can use
to help create the environment
in which we would like our children
and grandchildren to live.

Looking at today's world,
we very much need your help,
Spirit of Creation.

And yet we can have trust and hope.
Our grandchildren will have to struggle,
as we have and as our grandparents did;
yet through these struggles
they will adapt
to the environment in which they find
themselves.

The Past is Enfolded

Time doesn't pass;
It becomes enfolded into the present.

We know about dinosaurs
and the age of the reptiles
because their presence
is enfolded
in the skin of the Earth.

We know about 14.5-billion-year-old galaxies
because their light is enfolded in
the universe.
It can be seen today with our living eyes.

Recordings, CDs, and DVDs
are also examples.
All the sounds and pictures are always
contained in them.
We can hold them in our hands.
But for our limited senses and minds to
experience their contents,
it has to be presented
sound by sound and picture by picture
at the speed
at which it was originally recorded.

It can be presented faster,
as when the files are copied,
but we're incapable of understanding it.
It can even be copied all at once, instantly,
as in the case of vinyl records being stamped.

Prayer:

Divine Mother and Father,
Creator of all.

Time is there for us
and our limitations.

For you,
all is always present
and held in existence by you.

I need the time you give me
to live and breathe
and experience your gifts of love.

Thank you!

We know about
14.5-billion-year-old
galaxies
because their light is
enfolded in the universe.
It can be seen today with
our living eyes.

This star-filled image shows a star cluster: NGC 1866.

All is One

Not only is all one,
but all is also contained in all.
Think of Lady Julian's hazelnut.
"It's all here."

Look for the cloud in this sheet of paper.

Everything is contained,
in everything.
It cannot be separated.

While boundaries
help us to perceive and grasp,
and in some ways are real,
they are also an illusion.

There is no past or present.
And yet there is.

Everything is here, now,
contained in every other thing.

And God,
the Breadth of Creation
is present in all of it.

Prayer:

Spirit of Existence,
Help me to open my heart
to love all that exists,
especially my fellow humans.
The people that I will encounter this day.

Let Go

Let go;
I will catch you.

Let go
of the story
that you keep telling yourself.

You are so much more
than your story.

What am I hesitant to let go of?
Control.
I know I am not in control,
but I do like to
control
the situation and the people around me.

I like to drive the car.

I like to be the designated person in charge.

I decide when and how much I will exercise.

I wonder, is that control,
or is it using my gifts?

Prayer:

Spirit of Life and Love,
I place myself in your loving embrace.

You are the Creator
who brings forth
the next moment of existence.

Help me to use the gifts I have.
Enable me to share your message of love.

To Live is to Change

Evolution. A word for the ongoing process of creation. Everything is always changing. So everything is adapting to the new now.

History. A look back at what was. It's gone and cannot and will not return. So look back and learn the lessons it can teach. What are the vectors of change I can discern in myself? In my environment? In the world?

Vectors of Change. Arrows of creation. Which ones do I discern? And how am I going to interact with them? I can resist them, or I can recognize them, accept them, and try to adapt to them.

Prophets. Those who have the gift of seeing an arrow of creation. They are asked to call it to the attention of the world. They are not usually welcome. Their call is to help us see and change.

> I know what I know.
> It is locked into the cells
> of my brain and muscles.

It's hard work to change again,
and again,
and again.

Why does it go on,
and on,
and on?

Today is a good day.
Can't it last forever?

Prayer:

Spirit of Creation,
Give me the energy and the strength
to change again.
Thank you for today.
Lead me to tomorrow
with the lessons of yesterday.

Who am I?

Who was I before I was I, Me, Myself, Alan?

In the womb I existed, my heart beat, and my body developed. At some point in the time of my development, I was capable of surviving outside the womb, even though I was still not born.

After birth, I didn't know myself. It was only gradually that I came to recognize my name, Alan. If they had called me John, I would have responded to John. So am I Alan?

As I watch grandchildren and great-grandchildren develop, they are not separate. It takes time, growth, and experience for them to learn to exercise independence. To find the my — my ball, my bed, my plate, my food, my name. Who are they as they grow in independence?

I was before I was, and even though I can now say I am, that has not somehow made me independent or separated from all that is.

Prayer:

Spirit of Life,
Thank you for guiding me
on the road to self-recognition.

Please help me see even more clearly
that there is a wholeness
that came before me
and which holds me in existence.

A wholeness
which loved me into being.

Sparks

I am a spark
of human consciousness
in this vast created Universe.

The eye
by which I see God
is the eye
through which God sees me.

Eyes of God,
formed by life experience
in a human body,
observing the handiwork of the Creator.

And a bird flies by
a spark of bird consciousness,
and a dragonfly.

A tree,
blades of grass.

Prayer:

Thank you
for consciousness,
for eyes,
for growth,
experience and awareness.
Please help me to see you ever more clearly.

A Spark of Dragon Fly Consciousness

Passive vs Active Belief

As a child, I was told that I must believe what my community and my church believe. At liturgical services, we are asked to profess our beliefs. They even used the words believe and faith interchangeably. I believe that all this is passive belief. I also believe that to grow in faith, one must develop active belief.

Question the meaning of the statements we're told to believe. Kick it around, doubt it. Pray about it. Turn it over. If it's true, a deeper meaning and understanding will emerge. Faith is trust in the Divine, in the love of the Divine, which cannot be confined in human language.

The creeds, the commandments, the questions, and answers in the Catechism, and even the Scriptures, are the best efforts of those who have gone before me to share and explain their experiences of the Divine.

I am invited to enter into my relationship with the Divine. I need to recognize what I believe and arrive at my answers to the questions based on my experiences. And then to trust not in what I believe or understand but in the love that created me and holds me in existence.

Prayer:

Divine Love, Thank you for life.
Thank you for a mind that can question.
But after all the critical thinking,
I ask you to hold me in your love.

You loved me before I could think,
and I trust that your love will be there after thinking ceases.

The Incarnation

Incarnation is not an event,
but a continuous process.

Our Christian tradition remembers
and speaks of two incarnation events as
special stories.

The first is what we now call The Big Bang,
the bursting forth of the universe.

The second is the birth of Jesus.

But isn't every birth an incarnation?

Isn't God manifest
in the sprouting of every seed?

Prayer:

Spirit of Life,
Help me and all of us
to see and celebrate
your presence in all of creation.

The Kin-dom

The Kin-dom is here.
We just need to open the eyes of our inner being to recognize it.

From the very beginning,
and the very smallest
atoms are protons, neutrons, and electrons in relationship.

We don't understand it,
at least I don't,
the relationships that give rise to the
electron, proton, or neutron,
but we do know that there are energies in relationship.

The Dance of Creation — Evolution.

Compounds, cells, organs, organisms,
the living Earth dancing in relationship with
the Sun and other planets,
part of a galaxy dancing with other galaxies
in the universe of unmeasurable size.

Prayer:

Spirit of Creation,
Spirit of the Kin-dom,
Help me,
and all of us humans,
to grow
in our ability to see you
and to participate in the dance.

Time

God is doing something.
The Universe is in motion.
Things are changing.

Our God is writing a story
with the pen of time.

It's the story of creation.

A story of love outpoured.

A story of relationships.

A story of births,
deaths,
and transformations.

The finger of God
is writing another page
in the Book of Creation.

Prayer:

Hallelujah.
Thank you for writing
me
into your story
of creation.

Trees

Humans have built much
upon the face of Mother Earth.
But where would we be without trees?
Our buildings
make use of wood
from the trees.

Forests cover much of this planet.
Trees patiently make their contribution to
life.

Breathe in CO_2,
breathe out O_2,
and make the carbon into wood.

Prayer:

Thank you,
Brother and Sister Trees,
for all that you give us.

Lumber,
Fruit,
Nuts,
Shade,
Paper,
Clothing,
Maple Syrup,
Rubber,
Wind Breaks,
Fuel,
Board Walks ...

Humans have built much.
But where would we be
without trees?

The Messiness of Change

I just finished reading Ken Follett's, "A Column of Fire," about the Reformation and the Saint Bartholomew's Day massacre in Paris. What I find myself reflecting on is the messiness of change.

First, there is the process of growth and change in the individual. Then there is the process of the individual bringing their new understanding and attempting to affect society and the culture in which they live.

Each person sees the world with their own inner eye, shaped by society, religion, culture, and family values. Yes, some stir the pot, seeking personal gain, only adding to the pain and confusion. But many, I think most, are only trying to hold on to their own point of view. They see the whole messy process as a threat to that which they see as true and important.

Prayer:

Lord, help me
to seek multiple points of view.
And to hold all of them
loosely
so that the work you are doing
may be accomplished.

Peace in Chaos

This past year has been chaotic
in so many ways.
COVID,
political divisions and unrest,
storms, and fires.

And yet, my day-to-day life was peaceful.

I am reminded of Jesus in the boat,
asleep during the storm.

If we are trusting in our Creative God,
we can be at peace.

Storms, fires, and political unrest
are all signs
that creation is continuing.
Signs of change.

We,
the People of the Earth,
are living in a time of profound change.
Our creative God is at work.

But if I could ask my mother,
she would tell me
my birth was also a time of profound change,
pain, and bliss.

Trust!

Doubt

What is the relationship
between doubt and the voice of the spirit?

If I am open
— willing to be open —
the voice of the spirit,
gently,
over time,
leads me to doubt everything.
All lesser things —
all human understanding.

Prayer:

Spirit of Faith,
Help me not to fear doubt
but to trust.

Spiritual Experience and Religion

There's a complex relationship between
spiritual experience and religion.

On the one hand,
religion with its rituals,
language, and theological structures
can be a door to real spiritual experience.

However,
those structures and
the gatekeepers of the religious institutions,
can also misjudge and discourage growth,
invalidating and even condemning
not only the experience
but also
the person of the experience.

Prayer:

I thank you,
Spirit of Life,
for providing me
with companions grounded in religion
yet open to experience your leading and
wisdom.

Prayer

Conversation — Connection — Opening.

Prayer is never about changing God.
It's about changing me.
But since I live,
move, and have my being in God,
a change to me is a change to God.

Where is God?
At the core of all,
the ground of all being.

Being free,
able to make choices,
I can grow in awareness of God's Kin-dom,
or I can focus more on my individuality.
I can be a part of something more than me
and grow in that awareness,
or not.

Prayer:

Spirit of Life,
Continue to help me grow
in Kin-dom awareness.

Help me to grow in empathy
toward all in the family of Earth Life.

Autumn

The leaves have completed their work on behalf of the tree. Their chlorophyll has shut down and their sugars have been fed into the branches and trunk to be stored in the roots for the winter. We now see their true colors, and then one by one they will fall to the ground where they will add to the organic matter in the soil. The tree will stand naked until spring when new leaves burst forth from the buds.

We too are like leaves. We live for our season, one not defined by the orbit of the Earth. We add our gifts and abilities to the growth of the human family. When the time comes, we will shut down and hopefully recognize who we are, showing forth our colors as we complete our lives and allow ourselves to be transformed into the next stage of existence.

Prayer:

Spirit of Life,
Thank you for the privilege
of walking on planet Earth as a human.

Thank you for the people
who have been a part of my life,
the things I learned,
the work I was able to do,
and especially for bringing me together with
my life partner.

We too are like
leaves.
We live for our
season.

A version of the Lord's Prayer

Mother, Father, Creator God,
present in all relationships,
but always unnamed.

Help me to see your Kin-dom
ever more clearly.
Help me to open myself to your will
and the movements
of your creative spirit
in my life, and the community of Life on Earth.

Give me today the graces that I need.

Continue to teach me forgiveness,
for myself
and for all who have offended me.

Please do not test me beyond your grace,
but do lead me beyond all forms of
temptation.

Yours is this universe,
this planet Earth,
my home.
And to you, I give thanks, praise, and glory.
Amen.

There is More

*If there is no resurrection of the dead,
then even Christ could not have been raised.*
1 Cor 15:13

So, death is not an end,
any more than sleep at the end of day.

But what comes next?

What will follow this instant?

While we can use the past and the present
to "forecast the future,"
we really don't know
what comes next.

But nature, growth, scripture,
and experience
all teach clearly that more will come.

Prayer:

Thank you,
Spirit of Creation,
for giving me life and for showing all of us
that there is a resurrection.
Just as there is a spring to follow winter.

Guns and Bullets

This week, twenty-one students and teachers were shot at a school in Texas. Today, the NRA is starting its convention 300 miles away in Houston.

As a child, we had play guns. The easiest and the quickest was the pointed finger. We also used sticks.
We played cops and robbers,
and cowboys and Indians.

On a visit to Uncle Arnold's farm, I was permitted to shoot a BB gun at birds around the barn. However, I was caught pointing the gun at someone and all BB gun privileges were revoked. I don't recall ever shooting any gun after that.

But this isn't really about guns.
We can shoot at people with our prayers.
To fire off my will
and ask God or spirit energies
to change people
to my way of thinking is shooting at them.

Where is the loving embrace?

Where is listening?
Deep listening,
hearing their point of view.
Reflecting on it.
Considering it.

After all, isn't that what I want them to do
for me?

Yes, we all carry guns right in our fingers,
and we're capable of shooting divine energy
at those who think differently.

Prayer:

Spirit of Empathy and Compassion,
Open me,
help me to truly listen to all.

Do Trees Have Souls?

I was once asked if I thought trees had souls.
My answer was yes.
As I reflect further, I think,
and this is an opinion,
trees are a unique form of life.
All living things quickly become part of the
Milk of Earth Life*
once their life spirit is transformed through
death.

Their bodies feed other life forms.
Not so for all trees.

I am looking at a chair
made of wood from a tree.
Once the tree was alive;
you can see patterns of life
in the grain of the wood.

But now the tree soul has departed.
And yet the wood soul remains.
Yes, the tree, if left to rot and decay,
which is a slow process for many trees,
would become part of the
Milk of Earth Life.

I guess bones
and preserved life forms
would be similar.
However, I think trees are unique
and have two souls.

Prayer:

Spirit of Life,
Thank you for mystery
and a mind that can ponder mysteries.

*Milk of Earth Life:
From the moment of birth
we partake
and
become part
of this flow of life
in all its various forms
sharing life together
here on the Earth.

Wonder

The heavens declare the glory of God;
the skies proclaim the work of his hands.
Day after day they pour forth speech;
night after night they reveal knowledge.
They have no speech, they use no words;
no sound is heard from them.
Yet their voice goes out into all the earth,
their words to the ends of the world.
Psalms 19:1-4

I can marvel at a spectacular waterfall,
or an amazing sunset.

But do less attractive experiences stir wonder
in me?

Why are some born deaf?
Why is there war?
Why do storms and fires destroy?

When tragedy strikes,
do I stop and wonder?
Can I see my wondering as a wonder created
by God?

It seems that if I could learn to react this way,
it would open me.

Why is he this way?
Why did that occur?
Where is God in this?
I wonder?

Prayer:

Spirit of Wonder,
Grow in me.

The heavens declare the glory of God.

The skies proclaim the work of his hands.

Breath

The love of creation
flows to us in multiple vectors.

From the moment of creation,
it flows through all time and history.

From the creation of atoms,
it flows through the bonds of creation,
atoms, molecules, and all the levels and
forms of life.

As the universe expands,
it flows through space,
as light, gravity, and radio waves.

From the creation of DNA,
it flows through all life forms,
and all the generations of ancestors.

Prayer:

Breathe.
Draw it in from any
or all of the vectors.
And then breathe it out
to all the life forms surrounding you.

Layers of Life

Organic molecules, viruses, cells, bacteria,
organs, and organisms.
Life is in all of it.

Bonds,
working together,
a continuous web.

I find it interesting that life is passed to the
next generation
at the subcellular level.
Pollen, sperm, and egg.

A child is not conceived by its parents.
They start the process.
But who chooses the egg,
and the one of over thirty million sperm?

And from one cell,
newly made complete,
a new being develops.

Prayer:

Author of Life,
Thank you
for living through me.

Nobody

No Body. No Buddy. Nobody.

I've been looking at some of the pictures
from the new Webb telescope.
Wow, what a vast Universe.
And then here on planet Earth.
How many creatures?
How many billions of humans?

And where do I fit in this vastness?
I am little more than a nobody.

And yet, it is exactly the nobodies
that God loves.

I think of Jesus and the woman at the well.
She was there in midday
because she was a nobody,
an outcast in her community.
She was the life he touched and transformed.

God loves nobodies.
Newborn babies are nobodies,
but everyone loves them.
They are an example and a sign
of God's love.

Prayer:

Thank you
for the many times
you have touched my life.

A nobody
transformed by love.

Look at the dragonflies,
the monarch butterflies.

The flowers which fade tomorrow.

Love

My first thought is that love is a sentiment.

But isn't **All** love?

So how is the war in Ukraine love?
Sometimes we are too close,
and too affected by
the immediate conditions,
to see the workings of love.

Regardless of our immediate circumstances,
we can individually make loving decisions.

Individually, I can grow
in my understanding of self
and my neighbor.

When I get more time and space,
the process of transformation
associated with war may be easier to see.

The Civil War in this country
was part of a much larger movement,
opening the eyes of many
to the awareness that we are all
to be recognized and treated fairly and with
love.

Prayer:

Lord,
Open my eyes
to see
the presence of love in all.

May love be the root of my actions.

Parable of the Workers

It seems to me that the parable
of the workers in the vineyard (Mt 20:1-16)
is a metaphor for the spiritual journey.

Some wake up early in life
and spend a long time working in the
vineyard.

If they truly woke up,
it is a labor of great love and joy.

Others wake up later in life,
and spend less time,
but they still spent a lifetime searching.

And then some wake up
at the end of life.
Why?

Prayer:

Thank you for waking me up
and adding understanding
along the journey.

Church

When we say church,
what do we mean?
The institution(s)?
The Body of Christians?

Who is in the church, and
who and what are excluded?

I think back to my childhood,
a Catholic boy
with a non-Catholic mother.

A mother excluded.
And even today
most of the church's prayers
exclude the Mother.

It would be much more inclusive
to formulate prayers
for the whole human race,
regardless of church allegiance,
race, gender, status, or office.

Prayer:

Mother Goddess,
Bless us all,
hold us close this day.

Help us open our eyes,
and our hearts.

Prayers Change

Why did Jesus' disciples
have to ask him for prayer?

Our prayers,
our ways of praying
should not be static or set.
As we grow in our understanding
of ourselves and God,
our prayers can shift.

We can seek out new words,
new ways of sitting with the Divine.

That is not to discount
the prayers of our youth or
the Scriptures and the liturgy.
They will change more slowly;
they are there not just for me
but for the whole community.

Prayer:

Spirit of Life,
Keep helping me to grow.

But also keep me open
to accept all those I meet
as they are,
with their understanding and practices.

The Cloud's Prayer

Thank you for bringing me into being.

Fill me with moisture,
so that through me
you can water your creation.

Help me to pour myself out in tears,
tears of sorrow and joy,
as I blow over your garden,
seeing below me
the joys and sorrows of your people.

For this moment I am,
and so it is with your people,
today a joy to be followed by a sorrow
tomorrow.
They have a limited number of days on the
Earth.

Thank you for letting me see
your handiwork
and for allowing me,
just a puff of moisture,
to share myself, and participate
in this unfolding work.

May my tears turn sorrow to joy
and bring blessings upon your garden.

Acknowledgments

I wish to acknowledge those who helped me with this project. Without the suggestion from Sister Susan Kusz, SND, that I compile and share these reflections, this project would never have been started. Sister Anne Marie Lom, OSF reviewed this work several times and gave much-valued encouragement and advice. Marsha Rossiter provided reviews and helped me get started with the publishing process. Christine Keleny at CKBooks Publishing gave me the assistance I needed to complete the publication. Additionally, I am extremely grateful for the support, encouragement, and proofreading provided by my wife, Leanore.

About the Author

Alan Rommelfanger is retired and lives with his wife, Leanore, in Oshkosh, Wisconsin. They are the parents of six grown children. He enjoys daily walks, boating, and spending time with family and friends. Since retirement, his hobbies have been weaving, woodworking, cross-stitching, and reading.

In his young adult years, he spent some time in a religious community where he acquired the habit of daily prayer, meditation, and journaling. It is those lifelong habits that gave rise to these reflections.

www.ingramcontent.com/pod-product-compliance
Lightning Source LLC
Chambersburg PA
CBHW072052290426
44110CB00014B/1653